CURSED WITH A CURSE?

The Truth about Tithes and Offerings

Joy Allen, Ph.D.

ISBN: 069-2-382-2186
ISBN-13: 978-0-692-38218-9

DEDICATION

This book is dedicated first to God, then to all who are seeking truth in your pursuit of God; those who desire to know Him for yourself; those dedicated to Kingdom building and living a life of perpetual worship, pleasing to our Father. This is for you...

PROLOGUE

When determining God's will for His people, an in-depth study of the Scriptures is always an essential requirement. Tithing is an issue that has plagued the church for years, causing division between denominations, cultures and co-laborers in the Body of Christ. Why is this topic so divisive? Why are people so strongly opinionated in one direction or the other, yet generally ignorant about the history and purposes of the tithe?

While disappointing to acknowledge, we must be reminded that the love of money is indeed the root of all evil (1 Timothy 6:10). Church history is saturated with the preoccupation of wealth and status. With that, the tithe, which is often central to the acquisition of episcopal wealth, has taken on a life of its own. Many have taken the opportunity to capitalize off this doctrine, satisfying the insatiable desire for status and personal financial increase. While some struggle to ensure they are not cursed by failing to provide ten percent of their income to a church in religious institution, others take advantage of their ignorance and inability to demand from the same institution the rights that were awarded to those who paid the tithe throughout biblical history.

To uncover the truth about God's tithe, we must rely on His word, stripping away the culture and economic stance of today's local church. It is imperative that we, as much as possible, study the act of giving throughout the Word of God while also actively studying the context of each occurrence, to ensure a full understanding of God's overall divine plan and purpose.

Historically, God has created covenant patterns, which we often refer to as dispensations. Throughout time, each dispensation demonstrates His aim to reconcile His people back to Himself and build the church of Jesus Christ, based on a number of factors to include time, culture and the state of His people in relation to Him as God. We must all agree that the times, cultures, people and even our relationship with the Father has changed since the inception of the tithe. We can expect, then, that our Spirit-led relationship with the Father, through the blood of Jesus Christ, would certainly entail different expectations and requirements than that of Abraham or even the founding Apostles. Rightly dividing the word of truth, regarding this topic, will reveal that God's plans are never to burden His people without a purpose. In order to comprehend the purpose of tithing, both then and now, we must first understand God's will for His people in each dispensation of history where the tithe is present.

Contents

Acknowledgments

To my husband, Chris... You are my rock. I thank God for you and your willingness to push me into the destiny God has set for me. Your support and encouragement is priceless. I'm so in love with you!

To my children, Jaaron and Jasmine... You are my inspiration. Through you, God has demonstrated to me His unconditional love. You are both beautiful, anointed and destined for greatness. I love you with all my heart!

To my parents, Ronnie and Phyllis Rollins... Your love, kindness and encouragement have brought me this far. You've taught me that I can make a difference. I love you both, and I'm proud to be the "fruit of your labor."

To my Breath of Life family... You are truly the greatest church in the world. Thank you for the many prayers and words of encouragement. Most of all, thank you for trusting the God in me.

There are many others, in addition to these, who have supported me in writing and publishing this book. Thank you! Your love and prayers are appreciated.

INTRODUCTION

To tithe or not to tithe? **That is the question!**

Like so many, I was taught that the first ten percent of every penny I earned belonged to God. When I entered church without the appropriate amount, I found myself wondering what type of punishment I may have to endure. Conversely, when I did come prepared with my tithe, I was proud and arrogantly demanded, declared and decreed that I would be blessed... until I began to read the word of God for myself. After spending time in prayer and meditating on the word of God, I found that much of what I'd learned was merely unfounded. I noticed that many were being bound by a doctrine that was grossly misunderstood and negligently taught. After writing my Master's thesis on this very topic, I prayerfully set out to write an quick, easy to read book that would quickly present the truth of God's word regarding this topic, whereby many would be made free. This is that book.

For many years, scholars and saints alike have argued whether tithing should be mandated, taught or even practiced in the New Testament Christian church at all. Many teach that one's failure to give at least of tenth of all income to God, through the local church, results in a curse that persists regardless of one's lifestyle, motives or spiritual state. On the other side of the perpetual coin are those who completely dismiss the concept of tithing, concluding that the practice is outdated and often used as a tactic to coerce uneducated, unsuspecting believers into giving their money. To draw an appropriate conclusion, an in-depth study of God's word, and the history of His people is inevitable. The truth seeker must acquire an accurate biblical and historical understanding about not only the purpose of tithes and offerings, but the contextual chronicle that lends to that purpose.

At the center of every religious act, within the context of Christianity, is the concept of worship. Worship includes any biblically defined and divinely approved act of expressing adoration and reverence for God. The God we serve has a protocol for worship (1 Chronicles 15:13). We worship Him in Spirit and in truth, according to His own word and instruction. So then, it must be determined how, if at all, the paying of tithes fits into God's current protocol. Quite simply, is it what He desires from us? Is it a form of worship that He currently demands and accepts? If so, the conclusion is simple. Tithing must be mandated and practiced. If not, perhaps the practice should be reconsidered. After all, pleasing God, rather than man, must be our genuine motive.

For many, tithing is a very sensitive subject. Those who adhere to the doctrine of tithing are typically willing to give their last dime in order to defend the practice, while those who are opposed would do the same in favor of their argument. In fact, this concept is one of the most divisive beliefs in all of Christendom. It has created rifts between ministry colleagues and wars between denominations. How could a belief, based on the goodness of giving, be so divisive? At the core, it's simple. We cannot "rightly divide the word of truth" without knowing its author. No determination, involving an act of worship, can be made based only on history and repetition. It must be deducted within the realm of divine relationship and spiritual revelation.

Before reading the chapters of this book, I challenge you to step back for a moment. Forget your preconceived notions. Open your heart and mind not simply to another opinion, but to the facts as they relate to the heart of God. These facts will include a balanced combination of Scripture, history and a high level examination of God's character, based on His relationships with His people. The goal of this manuscript is to simply present the historical data and biblical framework required to draw a scriptural and spiritually sound conclusion. If you are ready for that adventure, one that will provide an objective overview and forever answer this very lively question – "To tithe or not to tithe!" Thank you for trusting the God in me as your tour guide. Now, grab your Bible and let's begin!

JOY ALLEN

WHAT IS THE TITHE?

Simply put, the term "tithe" means *a tenth* or 10%. Tithing is most commonly practiced in the Christian church as means of "giving back to God." Believers, in many arenas, are expected to give the first tenth of their income or earnings back to a local church, preferably the one they attend most regularly. This, in effect, signifies their obedience to the Word of God and their willingness to sacrifice for the work of the ministry.

Biblically speaking, the tithe is practiced and described under two of the seven dispensations – the dispensation of Promise with Abraham and the dispensation of law under the Mosaic covenant. Contrary to popular belief and widespread teaching, the practice of tithing began well *before* the Law and was likely practiced by pagans before used as an act of worship to Yahweh (Jehovah), the true and living God.

As with any moral or religious law or practice, dispensational understanding provides clarity on the purpose of each sacrament as it relates to a form of worship. A dispensation is simply "a method of interpreting history that divides God's work and purpose toward mankind into different periods of time[1]." In other words, dispensations are

---

[1] Got Questions Ministries, 2002-2014.
www.gotquestions.org

periods of time during which God communicates with His people, mandates worship and promises salvation in different terms. Most theological scholars agree that history can be divided into seven major dispensations: Innocence, Conscience, Human Government, Promise, Law, Grace and Millennial Reign (still to come). The dispensation of Promise, the first in which tithing is mentioned through Scripture, begins with the call of Abraham and continues until the Law of Moses is instituted. During this time, salvation is granted based on a belief in God's promises and a very selective calling, extended only to a few of His chosen people. In this era, Abram, later called Abraham, becomes the spiritual incubator through which God speaks to His people, interacts with nations and will later multiply His people in the earth. God's aim during this period is to multiply His seed of righteousness.

Tithing before the Law

Prior to the institution of the Mosaic Law, Scripture describes two separate occasions during which tithing is practiced. In the first instance, Abraham offers a tithe to Melchizadek following a victory in battle. Melchizadek, who some theologians identify as a spiritual prototype of Christ, is physically an honored king and priest of the Lord. Due to his victorious battle, Abram (Abraham) is blessed by the king. In response to the blessing of honor, the Bible tells us that Abram gives to the priest a tenth of his spoils from war, which he had taken from his victory over Chedorlaomer and his armies.

This tithe was not demanded or even solicited, but was in fact a practice Abraham would have seen and accepted through his access and influence from Babylonian culture and law. In many ways, it was like a love offering, a simple act of thanks and honor, given to the priest as a voluntary notion. It was a tip, of sorts, or could be interpreted as a voluntary tax to express gratitude and appreciation for support during the war. It's also important to note this tithe was not a repeated action. The gift was given once, due to the method in which they were collected and the cultural expectation for possessions taken in battle. There was no expectation for the gesture to be repeated systematically. Neither was the expectation inferred for others under the rule or lordship of this king and priest. Note this tithe had nothing to do with Abraham's personal possessions or increase from his own livelihood. Abraham was not a career soldier, but a herdsman who'd been blessed by God with tremendous wealth (Genesis 13). Yet, he did not present a tithe based on his increase aside from this battle.

After his [Abram's] return from the defeat and slaying of Chedorlaomer and the kings who were with him, the king of Sodom went out to meet him at the Valley of Shaveh, that is, the King's Valley. Melchizedek king of Salem [later called Jerusalem] brought out bread and wine [for their nourishment]; he was the priest of God Most High, And he blessed him and said, Blessed (favored with blessings, made blissful, joyful) be Abram by God Most High, Possessor and Maker of heaven and earth, And blessed, praised, and glorified be God Most High, Who has given your foes into your hand! And [Abram] gave him a tenth of all [he had taken].

Genesis 14:17-20, AMP

In the next instance, Jacob offers a tithe after receiving a visitation from God in a dream. The text suggests that this tithe was given voluntarily, without demand or solicitation. It was also presented as a sacrifice to God, without acceptance

18

by any man on His behalf. We can also assume, from the context of the Scripture, that tithing was not a regular practice for Jacob, but a gift or vow he decided to give based on a condition and personal agreement between him and God. It was a single covenant driven response to God's favor.

Then Jacob made a vow, saying, If God will be with me and will keep me in this way that I go and will give me food to eat and clothing to wear, So that I may come again to my father's house in peace, then the Lord shall be my God; And this stone which I have set up as a pillar (monument) shall be God's house [a sacred place to me], <u>and of all [the increase of possessions] that You give me I will give the tenth to You.</u>

Genesis 28:20-22, AMP

Considering the dispensation during which Jacob lived, the fact is that tithing is not required nor recommended at this time. The sacrifice is completely voluntary, before the institution of the Law, and not practiced regularly. It has no apparent purpose in God's focus for this dispensation – the multiplication of His people. The notable occurrence during the dispensation of Promise is that God's relationship with His people is solidified as He raises up a select few chosen vessels as leaders, conquerors and prophets for His Kingdom.

Many may wonder why, if the tithe was not instituted as law, Abraham and Jacob gave in this manner. Where did they get the idea? History chronicles that tithing was an ancient practice which existed long before Abraham. Ancient texts show evidence of tithing in a number of cultures, including those of Babylon, Egypt, Greece and Rome, prior to some of our earliest Hebrew texts. The original source is debatable, but we do know there was a cultural understanding already established by the time of Abraham, that ten percent of one's increase or material earnings, was an acceptable amount to give to a "higher" authority, as an act of honor, gratitude or respect. To some extent, we do know that such an offering was an established Babylonian law for political or military gain during the time of Abraham's victory. It is very likely that this cultural expectation influenced Abraham's actions, at least to some extent.

While many of our biblical studies of the tithe tend to be concentrated during periods of the Mosaic Law, the practice clearly existed as an honorable gesture well before this institution. In fact, the tithe was also existent within a number of pagan religions and cultures as an act of reverence or gratitude toward false gods and esteemed political or religious figures before it was ever adopted as a holy act of worship before the true and living God.

Even more, we can't ignore that tithing was not a monetary concept, though currency is clearly available and circulated during these times. Instead, as demonstrated in every biblical example, the tithe was comprised of possessions, mainly livestock and produce. This speaks loudly to the desire of God's people to honor covenant during the dispensation of Promise and the Law. They understood that any increase given by God, through covenant, can also be used to honor Him.

JOY ALLEN

Tithing Under the Mosaic Law

When God introduces the tithe as part of the sacred law for His people, He gives very specific instructions as to how the tithe should be presented and how it should be utilized. He also makes specific requests concerning what the tithe should consist of. Under the Law, the tithe included a host of agricultural items, including crops and livestock. Again, currency is not addressed. The first tenth of all increase was to be brought to God as a sacrifice, thereby defining the tithe as a sacrificial act of worship. Penalties were also put in place to increase the tithe in cases where instruction was not followed.

__And all the tithe of the land, whether of the seed of the land or of the fruit of the tree, is the Lord's__; it is holy to the Lord. And if a man wants to redeem any of his tithe, he shall add a fifth to it. And all the tithe of the herd or of the flock, whatever passes under the herdsman's staff [by means of which each tenth animal as it passes through a small door is selected and marked], the tenth shall be holy to the Lord. The man shall not examine whether the animal is good or bad nor shall he exchange it. If he does exchange it, then both it and the animal substituted for it shall be holy; it shall not be redeemed.

Leviticus 27:30-33, AMP

Generally speaking, the dispensation of Law begins with the establishment of the Law of Moses and continues until the death of Christ. During this dispensation, salvation is dependent upon obedience to God's law and His commandments. The Father establishes a priesthood to serve His now numerous people. It is indeed for this purpose that the tithe is established. The tithe is commanded, in part, to guarantee care and meet the needs of God's chosen priests, the Levites. The Levites were commanded to work in the temples and serve in ministry on behalf of God's people. This would inhibit their abilities to work, earn a living or support families as "normal" citizens. Consequently, the tithe was presented to them in exchange for their service before the Lord on behalf of His people. In exchange for their obedience to the priestly assignment, God ensured their needs were met through worship, then defined by the Law. He established and instituted the tithe, not only as a form of worship, but also as a very practical resource to meet the physical needs of the priests who ultimately gave their lives to the work of the ministry.

And, behold, I have given the Levites all the tithes in Israel for an inheritance in return for their service which they serve, the [menial] service of the Tent of Meeting. Henceforth the Israelites shall not come near the Tent of Meeting [the covered sanctuary, the Holy Place, and the Holy of Holies], lest they incur guilt and die. But the Levites shall do the [menial] service of the Tent of Meeting, and they shall bear and remove the iniquity of the people [that is, be answerable for the legal pollutions of the holy things and offer the necessary atonements for unintentional offenses in these matters]. It shall be a statute forever in all your generations, that among the Israelites the Levites have no inheritance [of land]. But the tithes of the Israelites, which they present as an offering to the Lord, I have given to the Levites to inherit; therefore I have said to them, Among the Israelites they shall have no inheritance. [They have homes and cities and pasturage to use but not to possess as their personal inheritance.]

Numbers 18:21-24, AMP

In addition to the institution of the tithe, God also establishes a number of feasts and rituals that must be practiced under the Law. His objective during this dispensation is to keep His people close to Him, that they would hear His voice and follow His direction. Obedience is now the key to right standing with God. It is the measure of one's holiness under the Law.

To ensure the feasts of the Lord were kept with ample substance, tithes were also commanded of the people for yet another purpose – their own consumption during Holy feasts whose observation

was required under the Law.   There were no
excuses for disobedience, so God, in His infinite
wisdom, built provision into His commandments
for the people.

*You shall surely tithe all the yield of your seed
produced by your field each year. And you shall eat
before the Lord your God in the place in which He
will cause His Name [and Presence] to dwell the
tithe (tenth) of your grain, your new wine, your oil,
and the firstlings of your herd and your flock, that
you may learn [reverently] to fear the Lord your
God always. And if the distance is too long for you
to carry your tithe, or the place where the Lord your
God chooses to set His Name [and Presence] is too
far away for you, when the Lord your God has
blessed you, Then you shall turn it into money, and
bind up the money in your hand, and shall go to the
place [of worship] which the Lord your God has
chosen. And you may spend that money for
whatever your appetite craves, for oxen, or sheep, or
new wine or strong[er] drink, or whatever you
desire; and you shall eat there before the Lord your
God and you shall rejoice, you and your household.
And you shall not forsake or neglect the Levite
[God's minister] in your towns, for he has been
given no share or inheritance with you. At the end
of every three years you shall bring forth all the
tithe of your increase the same year and lay it up
within your towns. And the Levite [because he has*

no part or inheritance with you] and the stranger or temporary resident, and the fatherless and the widow who are in your towns shall come and eat and be satisfied, so that the Lord your God may bless you in all the work of your hands that you do.

Deuteronomy 14:22-29, AMP

One interesting aspect about the tithe, which is often neglected or forgotten, is that the practice was intended to benefit the people, as well as the priests. In the book of Deuteronomy, we observe the first mention of money, or currency, as it relates to the tithe. Those people who were too far from the appropriate house of worship were permitted to sell their tithes of an entire year and use the money gained for travel and the purchase of meats for the feasts to be observed. Once again, while the tithe certainly had monetary value, it had to be translated into currency. The tithe itself remains an item of substance in the form of produce or livestock.

Another portion of God's plan dictates that every three years, the tithes were to be given cheerfully to the priests for a large feast, during which the poor and fatherless were invited to take part. As such, the tithe was purposed for worship, celebration and a means of biblical welfare – a system to care for the poor. While many churches today preach the tithe as a requirement, almost all fail to fulfill the converse obligations of the church, or "storehouse" that receives such gifts. In searching the church of today, it is likely none will be found that provide feasts for all the people in a community and commonly care for widows and orphans without cost, obligation or assistance from a local government. This division of the Law, where part is accepted while others are neglected, is due to a misunderstanding or lack of concern for God's original purpose of the tithe.

The pattern of God aiding His people by implementing laws and requiring their obedience has been established. It is clear that the tithe is not purposed to benefit God directly, but as a means to aid God's people in obeying Him and caring for one another. It is a method to eliminate excuse, ensuring that all who belong to the Father are included in the necessary acts of worship.

Malachi's Reference to the Tithe

The most well-known and commonly quoted scripture about tithing is found in the third chapter of Malachi. This Scripture, however, if not considered within the complete context of the prophetic text, can be and has been vehemently misunderstood and erroneously instructed.

Will a man rob or defraud God? Yet you rob and defraud Me. But you say, In what way do we rob or defraud You? [You have withheld your] tithes and offerings. You are cursed with the curse, for you are robbing Me, even this whole nation. Bring all the tithes (the whole tenth of your income) into the storehouse, that there may be food in My house, and prove Me now by it, says the Lord of hosts, if I will not open the windows of heaven for you and pour you out a blessing, that there shall not be room enough to receive it. And I will rebuke the devourer [insects and plagues] for your sakes and he shall not destroy the fruits of your ground, neither shall your vine drop its fruit before the time in the field, says the Lord of hosts. And all nations shall call you happy and blessed, for you shall be a land of delight, says the Lord of hosts.

Malachi 3:8-12, AMP

This prophetic declaration is a directive given to the Levitical priests, who had sinned against God, along with the people of Israel. The account described notes that Israel was punished due to their disobedience demonstrated by offering sick and lame animals to God. The prophet Malachi is speaking to the priests about God's anger and the things they would need to do in order to reverse the curse currently upon them, which came due to their disobedience and deceptive attempts to cheat God by keeping the best portions of the peoples' offerings for themselves (Malachi 1:6-8). In exchange for their repentance and future obedience, God vows to replenish their land, bless the people and rebuke the devourer, which is literally the reverse of the pestilence and famine they suffered due to sin and deception. This sin is what caused God to reject their sacrifices of worship. Like any other portion of Scripture, an understanding of the entire book of Malachi will clearly reveal context of this Scripture and the audience to whom it is addressed. As a matter of fact, the directive in Malachi is not intended for a general audience in regard to tithing, but specifically to those priests who violated the tithe through their own evil acts, as they purposely sacrificed to God the sick and lame while preserving the best for themselves.

Tithing Foundations

Though the book of Malachi is the most commonly quoted reference to tithing, there are actually three purposes of the practice recorded under the Law, none of which are directly mentioned in this text. Everything God requires of His people is ultimately for one divine purpose – reconciliation. Our Father is not a dictator who enjoys belaboring His people with meaningless tasks, nor is He an egotistical politician who desires to hoard those things earned by others. Instead, He is a loving and just God, who since the fall of man, has implemented a number of spiritually corrective actions designed to bring His people back to Him. His desire is to restore man back to the perfect and sinless state once present in the Garden of Eden. His goal is to, once again, make us like Him.

To promote this intention, God executes the tithe with a three-fold existence and purpose under the Law. As already established, and now reiterated, that purpose includes:

- the support of the Levitical priesthood,
- the celebration of sacred feasts, and
- the support of the poor and widows.

Reverting back to our original question as to whether or not the tithe is essential for the New Covenant believer, it is important to examine these needs, which God met with the requirement of the tithe. Do these needs exist today? If so, are they met by the tithe in our current practice? If not, how effective is an act of worship that fails to meet God's purpose and expectation for that act? Selah.

Is Tithing for the New Testament Church?

It is evident, through the history Jesus' ministry, the people failed to meet all the needs which would have been addressed through an obedient practice of tithing. The widespread corruption within the church ensured the priests were taken care of, though feast celebrations and care of the poor were certainly not up to par with God's expectations. The same disconnect seen today was evident even then. The law became a doctrine of control and coercion rather than one of worship and social benefit. Even in the midst of the corruption and turmoil, Jesus rarely mentions tithing during His earthly ministry. The Scriptures do not provide proof that tithing is clearly commanded or even mentioned as a recurring practice of His disciples or the founding Apostles. The Bible is clear that with His crucifixion, Christ completes the Law, and thereby completes and concludes the era of the Levitical priesthood, catapulting us into what theologians call the Dispensation of Grace.

Dispensational grace begins with the resurrection of Jesus Christ and will remain until the return of our Savior. Salvation, in this era, is obtained by being born again, resulting from the confession and belief in Jesus Christ as Lord and

Savior. Believers must "take up their cross," and follow Him, whether Jew or Gentile. As such, the tithe cannot seemingly persist or endure in the exact same manner it was practiced, as many components of the institution are no longer valid, relevant or required for right standing with God (i.e. high priests, rituals, etc.). This includes animal sacrifices and the observance of religious festivals and feasts under the Law. After all, salvation is now extended to both the Jew and the Gentile (Romans 2:10-11; 9:24; 1 Corinthians 12:13). Gentiles, of course, would not have met the qualifications of a law previously inclusive of only the Hebrew nation.

Let us remember that God sets in place requirements for a divine purpose. The original intent of the tithe was in part to care for a priesthood which has now been extended to include all who belong to the Body of Christ (1 Peter 2:9-10). So, is the Law for today? If so, is the tithe a part of the Law? We've established already that tithing existed, and was honored (or received) by God prior to the Mosaic Law. We understand that Jesus completes the Law of Moses, but doesn't destroy or nullify it (Matthew 5:17). What does this mean for those of us who are now part of the New Covenant, living in the dispensation of grace?

The Mosaic Law can be dissected into three parts, or categories: Civil Law, Ceremonial Law and Moral Law. Civil law is concerned with the private interactions within a community. It speaks to the way a society handles itself on a daily basis while ceremonial law deals with religious practice and ritual. The rituals and rites described within the ceremonial law, or religious culture, must be completed in order for an individual to obtain and maintain favor with God. Evidently, Jesus Christ completed both the civil and ceremonial requirements of the Law through His shed blood. As such, society now handles itself differently. For instance, it's no longer required that a witch be stoned or every young boy be circumcised in order for a town or country to obtain God's favor. From a ceremonial perspective, the sacrifice of animals is no longer required for the remission of sin. Jesus fulfilled the requirements to free His born again followers from these stipulations. Nevertheless, moral law remains as defined by the Father. Moral law provides guidance on holiness – activities that are accepted or rejected by God. We know that Jesus preached the moral law of God, because moral law reflects God's very nature, which has not and will not change throughout the dispensations. It is around moral law that our ethics are defined. Murder has been and will always be wrong. The same remains, for example, of adultery, blasphemy, theft, etc.

The tithe, though it clearly existed prior to the Mosaic Law, was later adopted as part of the civil law through Moses. Some may even argue that it should be considered as part of the ceremonial law. Either way, the Messiah completed the work of both with His death and resurrection, freeing us from the bondage to either. Based on this liberation, the tithe cannot be a valid requirement under this dispensation of grace, as the law of ceremony or civilization must stand or fall as a unit. We cannot feasibly maintain the validity of some portions while excusing others (James 2:10). Furthermore, the tithe is no longer needed as a means or tool of reconciliation back to the Father, which has been God's desire for every dispensation of time. Jesus bridges that gap, as reconciliation now takes place through Christ the Messiah and He is the only way to connect to God (John 14:6, 1 Timothy 2:5-6).

Tithing in the New Testament

Tithing is neither clearly condemned nor encouraged by Jesus or the New Testament Apostles in Scripture, though it is clearly not applicable as an enforceable law for those who have been adopted into the family of God through our resurrected Messiah.   Nevertheless, tithing both before and within the context of the Law was favored and accepted by God as a set standard of worship. While the law is clearly inapplicable, the principle must be considered by the New Testament believer, simply because it has always pleased God.   Is it possible to do that which is not required by a religious law to please God in this dispensation of grace?

Altogether, tithing is mentioned just six times in the New Testament, though it is never commanded nor condemned.   The only aspect ridiculed is an attention to tithing, by the Pharisees, without a heart focus on more important matters of God's Kingdom.

Woe to you, scribes and Pharisees, pretenders (hypocrites)! For you give a tenth of your mint and dill and cummin, and have neglected and omitted the weightier (more important) matters of the Law—right and justice and mercy and fidelity. These you ought [particularly] to have done, without neglecting the others.

Matthew 23:23, AMP[2]

Even as Jesus addresses the tithe, it must be considered that each of His references is within the context of law throughout the New Testament. It is not suggested as an open practice for anyone outside the Law, including those covered by the grace extended to Gentiles. We can conclude clearly that the death, burial and resurrection of Jesus completed the letter of the law for believers under grace, so it is not surprising that Jesus, during His ministry on earth, would address the Law in the context of Jewish leaders, as it was still being practiced until His disciples established His church, following the resurrection. It is this New Covenant church, after receiving power to do so by the Holy Ghost (Acts 1:8), that openly preaches salvation to all without the requirement of converts to fulfill the tenets of the Law.

Consider for a moment, Jesus' reference to tithing of mint, dill and cumin. It should be noted that even in this New Testament reference, the tithe exists within the context of produce, rather than currency. This is interesting, as we know that currency, while perhaps not in circulation during some of the Old Testament references, is certainly available and widely used during the time of the Messiah's earthly ministry (Matthew 22:19-21). Yet,

---

[2] See also Luke 11:42; 18:12

the tithe in this single reference by Jesus does not deal with money at all, rather substance.

Another New Testament reference seemingly provides a directive for *descendants of priests to receive a tithe*, as mentioned in the book of Hebrews.

And it is true that those descendants of Levi who are charged with the priestly office are commanded in the Law to take tithes from the people—which means, from their brethren—though these have descended from Abraham. But this person who has not their Levitical ancestry received tithes from Abraham [himself] and blessed him who possessed the promises [of God].

Hebrews 7:5-6, AMP[3]

Interestingly enough, this Scripture highlights the directive for descendants of Levi to receive the tithe from God's people. The author, widely believed to be the Apostle Paul, then expounds on Abraham's gift to Melchizedek, but again neglects to provide instruction for the New Covenant believer. The chapter goes on to explain the priesthood of Christ and His superiority to Melchizedek as priest, noting that the Levitical priesthood was weak and unable to bring everlasting salvation. Jesus Christ, however, offers a

---

[3] See also Hebrews 7:8-9

"better covenant" with God, superseding that of the Law. In essence, the system and government of Christ is more effective than that which pre-existed Him – the same system and covenant that included the tithe. At the foundation of this covenant lies the premise of blood sacrifice (Hebrews 9:22), which Jesus forever filled and satisfied by becoming the final sacrificial Lamb (Matthew 26:28). It is now our job, as New Covenant believers, to maintain right standing with God through worship, as led by the Holy Spirit.

Grace Giving

The New Testament focus, for the Church of Jesus Christ, is on "grace" giving or free-will offerings. Forced, law-driven giving is not commanded or encouraged by Jesus, nor is it mentioned in the Epistles, which are blueprints for church conduct and activity, as contributed by the original Apostles. The Apostle's doctrine clearly never establishes or enforces the tithe.

Throughout the book of Acts, which chronicles the establishment of Christ's church and the patterns of giving (Acts 2-6), people shared what they had with others freely, in obedience to a joint expectation, though not a law or forced mandate (Acts 4:32). "From time to time" (Acts 4:34), they also gave possessions to support those in need, as observed in the case of Barnabas (Acts 4:34-37) who sold a field he owned and brought the profits to the apostles. We can observe, through these examples, that the same needs are met for which the tithe was originally established, to include the care of God's people, provision for godly fellowship and care for the needy. Yet, the tithe is not solicited. Instead, God's people are led by His Spirit, which indwells every born-again believer, to meet needs through giving, without observing the letter of the Law.

In short, the law of tithing does not seemingly apply to the New Testament church, yet the purposes of the tithe – the responsibility of believers to care for the church, one another and the needy – are very much alive! Sacrificial giving is the *principle* behind tithing. This is what pleases God. While the substances being sacrificed have evolved with time, the concept of consecrated sacrifice has always been a staple of worship (Psalm 51:16-17). Consider, for example, singing and dancing as acts of worship. Like tithing, both were established and practiced under the Mosaic Law. Jesus, as with tithing, doesn't clearly encourage nor condemn worship through song, dance or the use of instruments. Yet, these practices continue. They are not regimented by law, but accepted by God as they are freely offered. The need for worship must still be fulfilled, and we understand through Scripture and biblical history that these methods of worship are pleasing to God. In like manner, we are able to draw similar conclusions about the tithe, now as a pattern for free worship rather than a requirement of the Law.

It is true that we are no longer bound by the Mosaic Law, to which the traditional concepts of tithing belong. We no longer gather barns of grain and sacrifice to prepare for feasts. Nor do we support a Levitical priesthood. We do, however, have a responsibility to understand and preserve the principles and patterns of worship that have been presented in the Word of God, as they were obviously accepted by our Father through the dispensations.

CURSED WITH A CURSE?

As we examine the giving demonstrated in the New Covenant church, many would note that the level of sacrificial giving, in most cases, seems to "outweigh" a simple tithe. In our Scriptural examples, most gave their all, or were at least willing to sacrifice as much as was needed in a given situation. It is clear that God is more concerned with the heart of the giver than the amount. In the example of Ananias and Sapphira (Acts 5), for example, the husband and wife were not punished by death due to the amount they gave or refused. Instead, it was due to the state of their hearts. They lied to the Holy Ghost, attempting to deceive rather than give with a pure heart of sacrifice.

The responsible reaction for the New Covenant church then is to honor the *principle* of tithing (sacrificial giving for the support of ministry, fellowship and the poor) rather than preserving a religious ritual. The heart of the giver (which must respond to the principles of acceptable worship) rather than the amount, is emphasized. A principle is merely "a fundamental truth or proposition that serves as the foundation for a system of belief or behavior." Biblical principles govern the life of every believer, though we operate under grace and are not bound by law. Sacrifice, priesthood, worship and even prayer were all once part of the Law, dictated by protocol. We are free from dictation and protocol, now operating out of a changed heart and a new Spirit (John 3:4-6). We are now **free** to worship and do so out of love rather than obligation. These same concepts – sacrifice, priesthood, and worship – are not neglected, but observed from a heart of love and obedience rather than one of compulsion, duty or fear (Psalm 51:16-17).

The Body of Christ can confidently claim we all are priests, by grace (1 Peter 2:9). We are accepting of the doctrine that we must become living sacrifices, by grace (Romans 12:1-2). These principles are not foreign to us, though they now reside on a spiritual foundation of faith, rather than a natural foundation resulting from command. The responsibility of Christ's followers is to understand and observe the *principles* of tithing (rather than the tithe itself), by faith through grace. God's nature has not changed. The benefits we enjoy by grace are indeed based on the Law. Plainly stated, we reap the benefits of grace *because of* the Law (Galatians 2:21; 3:11; 5:4).

Tithing, under grace, is no longer a requirement, but presents a *principle standard* or spiritual basis of giving. It is a blueprint or guidance, not to be misinterpreted as a means to abundance nor a route to destruction if not practiced. One may indeed argue that any true, generous giver, led by the Holy Spirit, will not have any quarrel or concern with giving ten percent of their income or increase to a church, ministry or charity. In our freedom from the Law, grace will allow the conviction of the Holy Spirit to instruct us to give with a willing and cheerful heart. It is indeed our responsibility to be led of the Holy Ghost, using the tithe as a measuring rod to ensure we remain sensitive to His instruction.

JOY ALLEN

THE PURPOSE OF GIVING

Quite simply, giving is our responsibility as Christians, because it is commanded by God. Those who love our Heavenly Father will follow and obey His commandments. Frankly, those who love God, then, will never have a problem giving. It is part of our Christian service as an act of worship. It is the vehicle through which God blesses His people (2 Corinthians 9:10).

Every principle of God points back to worship. The ability to give and the act of giving are blessings, because they honor God.

In everything I have pointed out to you [by example] that, by working diligently in this manner, we ought to assist the weak, being mindful of the words of the Lord Jesus, how He Himself said, It is more blessed (makes one happier and more to be envied) to give than to receive.

Acts 20:35, AMP

So then, as occasion and opportunity open up to us, let us do good [morally] to all people [not only being useful or profitable to them, but also doing what is for their spiritual good and advantage]. Be mindful to be a blessing, especially to those of the household of faith [those who belong to God's family with you, the believers].

Galatians 6:10, AMP[4]

In addition to giving as a mere act of worship, with a heart to please God, we must remember that even in the dispensation of grace, there is a need to support men and women who are called and ordained to full-time, or vocational ministry, and have dedicated their lives to Christian service. Very real needs exist, and God has always been pleased by seeing such needs met, so that His work can go forth.

Now concerning the money contributed for [the relief of] the saints (God's people): you are to do the same as I directed the churches of Galatia to do.
1 Corinthians 16:1, AMP

Now about the offering that is [to be made] for the saints (God's people in Jerusalem), it is quite superfluous that I should write you;
2 Corinthians 9:1, AMP

[On the same principle] the Lord directed that those who publish the good news (the Gospel) should live (get their maintenance) by the Gospel.
1 Corinthians 9:14, AMP[5]

---

[4] See also Acts 2:44-45; 1 John 3:17; Galatians 6:9-10

[5] See also 1 Timothy 5:17-18; 1 Corinthians 9:6-14; Philippians 5:15-18

The truth of the matter is that Christian giving is God's way of funding the work of the church, including care for the poor and provision for the saints. This has never changed. Tithing under the Law provided for these needs throughout the Mosaic covenant, and free will giving, with tithing as a precursor, is meant to do the same in the covenant of grace.

Jesus Christ, in fulfilling the Law, gave us a more excellent, or a better, covenant (Hebrews 8:6). This means we are not required to follow the letter of previous agreements with God. He understood that something better was needed, and therefore sent His only Son, Jesus Christ, to establish a new covenant with His people. As with every other letter of the Law, the tithe could not sanctify or change the hearts of God's people. The tithe is powerless to bring forth salvation or redemption. It cannot cleanse or make new. Its purpose, under the *better* covenant, is to provide a spiritual blueprint for an acceptable type of worship, namely proportional, sacrificial giving. By demanding a percentage of one's increase, our Heavenly Father guaranteed that everyone gave a fair share. A percentage is automatically proportional, with an expectation that those who earn more will give more. This concept of proportional giving, along with sacrificial giving, is another tithing principle that is expressed in the

New Covenant church initiated by the founding apostles.

GIVING IN THE NEW TESTAMENT CHURCH

First and foremost, Christian giving should not be reduced only to money. David proclaimed that he would never give anything to God that did not cost him something (2 Samuel 24:24). In the same manner, our giving is an act of worship and should require sacrifice. That sacrifice must consist of more than money alone. God desires our time, talents and work for Kingdom building (Romans 12:1-2; 1 Corinthians 6:19-20). One who feels they can gain and maintain the grace of God with money alone has indeed not been born again and does not carry within himself the Spirit of God. Money is only one of many sacrifices we are expected to present to our Heavenly Father. It pertains only to a small percentage of commandments we are required to follow.

In reference to financial giving, the Bible teaches purposeful, planned and proportional personal giving for the New Testament church. Many specific instructions are provided regarding *how* a Christian should give. These instructions should be observed by all believers in reference to giving.

Personally (1 Corinthians 16:2)

- Each can only give what he or she has. Our financial giving is based on our own earnings, rather than that of another or any amount contributable to a loan or credit.

Planned, faithfully, systematically (1 Corinthians 16:1-2)

- The Word of God instructs us to follow a procedure in regard to our giving. We must contemplate our earnings and consciously set aside an amount to give. We often see a strong contradiction to this teaching in our modern-day "emotional" offering services. Prior to coming into the house of God, the believer should have a gift set aside for giving.

Purposefully (2 Corinthians 9:6-7)

- Giving should not be an accident or an emotional reaction. The Word of God encourages the believer to make considerations and give with a purpose in mind.

Proportionally (1 Corinthians 16:2; Acts 11:29; 2 Corinthians 9:11)

- It is not God's intention to place a financial burden on His people. As the tithe established the principle of proportional giving, God extends the same in the realm of New Testament giving. We give proportionally, according to our increase and ability.

Joyfully (2 Corinthians 9:6-7)

- We know and understand that God loves a cheerful giver. Giving should never be laborious. Believers should not be forced, coerced or "guilted" into giving. Like any form of worship, we give freely and should be happy to do so.

Gratefully (2 Corinthians 9:15)

- Thanksgiving must always be the backbone of our giving. We give to God as a sign of our gratefulness for all He has already done.

Voluntarily; not under compulsion (2 Corinthians 8:2-4; 9:7)

- God's people must give freely and according to one's own will and conviction. Under the dispensation of grace, God is not interested in forcing anyone to give out of compulsion. He is looking for those who will worship Him in Spirit and in truth. He is looking for relationship with His people. Giving, in such a relationship and as an act of pure worship is done voluntarily by one who simply wants to demonstrate their love for

God through giving. With that, no one should ever give due to pressure, compulsion or fear. Giving should be a pleasurable experience!

Sacrificially (2 Corinthians 8:1-5)

- As David vowed to give God only that which required something of himself, we should do the same in the Lord's church. Giving should be sacrificial, in that it requires some discomfort that we are willing to endure to demonstrate our love. Every healthy relationship includes some compromise. Our relationship with God is no different. Giving allows us an opportunity to show Him how much we are willing to sacrifice for Him.

Anonymously (Matthew 6:1-4; Acts 5:1-11)

- According to the Scriptures, those who give openly to receive the applause of men have received their reward. The New Testament church is called to give anonymously, without the desire for approval by men, based on our gifts. Financial giving, like any other form of worship, should have an audience of one – the One. It is a private act between that individual and God. It is not something that should be monitored, reviewed or audited by another. Once anonymity is compromised, the giver will likely cater to pleasing the flesh or oneself or another, rather than the Father.

Compassionately (Luke 6:30-31)

- Every believer must have compassion. The Bible states the world will know we are Christians by our demonstration of love. Believers demonstrate this love for others by giving to the poor and needy. Just as we are able to ask of our Father, others should be able to ask of us in times of need. Giving, for the New Covenant church, extends beyond the local church or God's called leaders. We have a responsibility to give to our community as well.

Expectantly (Luke 6:38; 2 Corinthians 9:6; Proverbs 19:17; 1 Timothy 6:18-19)

- Giving, as an act of faith, is tied to a number of biblical promises. Therefore, when we give, we should do so with expectation, believing that God will reward our giving according to His Word. Giving is an act of faith, and every act of faith is tied to a supernatural result. According to Scripture, seedtime and harvest will exist throughout the existence of the world (Genesis 8:22). When we give, we can expect God to continue blessing us, though this should not be our motive. Remember, it's the heart of the giver (rather than the gift itself) that God sees and considers. We will indeed reap what we so (2 Corinthians 9:6; Galatians 6:7-9).

As observed, the underlying principles of tithing are translated into Paul's teachings on how a Christian should give. The concept of giving God the first and the best is highlighted in his instruction to "set aside" money at the beginning of each week, or a set time. The underlying theme of giving proportionate to one's income is also stressed, which is the framework upon which tithing was laid. When these gifts are saved up and presented according to the Word of God, according to Paul's plan as it also sufficed with the tithe of the Law, extra collections, coercion and fund raisers will not be needed to care for God's messengers, the house of God, nor the surrounding community.

In essence, tithes are paid under the Law. Under grace, we worship through giving. We give unto God, as a part of our worship. It is unto God, not man (1 Chronicles 16:29). Every believer, then, should welcome any opportunity to give, especially to God. Giving grants God an avenue by which to bless us, according to His word. In like manner, the tithe brought a blessing to God's people – both those who gave and those who received the gift.

STEWARDSHIP PRINCIPLES

The truth is this – It takes money to run a church or ministry. It takes money to meet the needs of God's people. Finances are required to meet the needs of the poor and our communities. Money is still the answer to all things (Ecclesiastes 10:19). Quite simply, our giving helps to extend the hand of God in the earth, because the resource we give help to fund the work of the ministry. When men see these good works, they will glorify our Father (Matthew 5:16). Those who enjoy giving do not have a problem giving to a "cause" they believe in. If one is not comfortable giving to their perspective church or ministry, that person should take inventory of their own motives and the work of that church or ministry. If a resistance to giving exists, perhaps the problem is rooted in the knowledge that a particular institution is not doing enough for the Kingdom of God. Oftentimes, we are told to give unto God and hold no regard to what happens thereafter. This thinking is actually contrary to the Word of God.

Stewardship is "the act or job of protecting and being responsible for something." A good steward is one who watches over their resources and applies them in responsible ways. With the intention of being a good steward over what God has given us, we need to know the proper use of our money and gifts, according to the Scriptures. It is our responsibility to sow time, money and resources where the work of the Kingdom is being done. That target may be variable over time. And though it should include our own house of fellowship, it may not in every instance. It is also the responsibility of a good steward to ensure that sensible decisions are made concerning the resources with which God has equipped us. It is the sower who continues to receive seed from God (2 Corinthians 9:10), and His desire is that our seed be planted in good ground. It is a seed planted in good ground that produces good fruit, which is required to please God (Matthew 13:23; 25:14-28; John 15:1-2). Contrary to what many believe, it is the giver's responsibility to judge "the soil."

Of course, we are to give to the work of the ministry and those in need. Additionally, a good steward is required to take appropriate responsibility for his or her own family. Responsibility is an expectation of those belonging to Christ's church. Responsible giving and strong stewardship ensure we meet this expectation. God's expectation is that we not be a burden to the church, especially when we are able to care for ourselves. This can only be accomplished when we are faithful over our own homes and business affairs. Aside from the poor and widows, or the like, believers should not expect benefits from the local church. In addition to giving, we are expected to care for ourselves as much as possible, freeing the local church or fellowship to truly care for those in need.

__If anyone fails to provide for his relatives, and especially for those of his own family, he has disowned the faith [by failing to accompany it with fruits] and is worse than an unbeliever [who performs his obligation in these matters].__ Let no one be put on the roll of widows [who are to receive church support] who is under sixty years of age or who has been the wife of more than one man; And she must have a reputation for good deeds, as one who has brought up children, who has practiced hospitality to strangers [of the brotherhood], washed the feet of the saints, helped to relieve the distressed, [and] devoted herself diligently to doing good in every way.

1 Timothy 5:8-10, AMP

Good stewards, according to the Word of God, also ensure the needs of their household are met, even when considering how they will give. Personal debts and household expenses are prioritized with a faithful giver – one who is a good steward. Simply put, if we strive to be faithful over that which God has given us, we will **pay our bills**! Regardless of what we give at our local church, those who do not pay their own debts are described as evil and disobedient by God. Interestingly enough, those who fail to care for their households are scripturally chastised much more harshly than those who fail to give to a church or ministry. We need to work and fulfill our financial obligations, as our Father has this expectation of us. It is just as important and giving in terms of worship and righteous living.

Render to all men their dues. [Pay] taxes to whom taxes are due, revenue to whom revenue is due, respect to whom respect is due, and honor to whom honor is due.

Romans 13:7, AMP

For while we were yet with you, we gave you this rule and charge: If anyone will not work, neither let him eat.

2 Thessalonians 3:10, AMP

The wicked borrow and pay not again [for they may be unable], but the [uncompromisingly] righteous deal kindly and give [for they are able].

Psalm 37:21, AMP

A true, born-again believer with a heart for ministry will never willingly become a burden to the church. This includes ministers and leaders. Each servant of God has the responsibility to accept gifts of God's people only when acceptance will not retard the work of the ministry. For example, pastors who quit their secular jobs to demand salary from a local assembly, thereby placing upon them a financial burden are operating outside of wisdom and the Scriptural guidance provided by Paul. The apostle, who also worked as a tent maker, assisted in the support of his ministry assignments on various occasions. This conservatism is further expressed by Paul in his letter to the Corinthian church announcing his upcoming visit.

Now for the third time I am ready to come to [visit] you. And I will not burden you [financially], for it is not your [money] that I want but you; for children are not duty bound to lay up store for their parents, but parents for their children.
2 Corinthians 12:14, AMP

Finally, a good steward understand God's will for his or her life. We must be able to recognize the purpose for money, in seed form. Believe it or not, every ordinance and commandment given by God is for our own good. His goal, since the beginning of time, has been to bring His creation into a perfect world of enjoyment with Him. God wants us to enjoy life! In our giving, we remember that enjoying the fruit of one's labor is not sinful, but encouraged (Ecclesiastes 5:18-19). As such, we must never give out of a false sense of responsibility to "suffer." As a matter of fact, it's perfectly okay to use your money to treat yourself every now and then. There is no sin in using one's income to pamper themselves, in moderation, so long as the support of ministry is not forsaken (Haggai 1:4).

As for the rich in this world, charge them not to be proud and arrogant and contemptuous of others, nor to set their hopes on uncertain riches, but on <u>God, who richly and ceaselessly provides us with everything for [our] enjoyment.</u>

1 Timothy 6:17, AMP

Giving is the ultimate worship opportunity. It is also the best insurance plan of all, as to give without reciprocation is impossible, according to the biblical promises of God.

DOCTRINAL ACCURACY

We understand that every good and perfect gift comes from our Heavenly Father (James 1:17). Therefore, we celebrate our gifts, both natural and spiritual, and make every attempt to use them in worship. Our desire is to provide God a return on His investment. Our prayer is that our gifts will be offered in excellence and accepted by our Father.

We should celebrate and welcome every opportunity to worship, which includes financial giving. Giving should provide the occasion to execute an exciting act of love toward God. As giving is a part of worship, it should take place at a time when God's people are collectively praising Him through song, dance, hand clapping, and anything else purposed to glorify God (Psalm 54:6; Hebrews 13;15). Just as other forms of worship are corporately performed, yet personally offered, our giving should be also. Worship must always be free, driven by a pure motive. Purity of heart, unfortunately, is automatically compromised when force is implemented.

The *principles* of tithing should be encouraged and actively practiced, not as an act of the Law, but as a godly standard expressing the proportionate sacrifice and accountability (Romans 3:31; 7:7). Tithing, for the believer, is merely a benchmark, or a measuring stick, that has been set throughout the Word of God and history to teach the appropriate attitude of worship through giving. It existed well before the Law, so we can accept the purpose without yielding to the "bondage" of ritual. Freewill giving, placed upon the foundation of tithing, is a grace principle. We do not "pay" tithes, but we gladly "give" above and beyond a mere tithe, or anything else He requests, unto the Lord. We do so freely, with a grateful heart, without fear of retaliation or punishment from God. It is without fear of being cursed or any other coercion or bribery. We are not to tithe nor teach it in a legalistic manner, measuring every exact cent. We are, instead, to utilize the tithe as a guide in obeying the New Covenant instructions for giving.

We acknowledge there may very well be times when an emergency arises. It is not God's expectation that we neglect the needs of our home or family to meet the obligation of a tithe. Instead, we understand that the grace of God covers us in those times. God has given us the resource we need to handle the matter. One who practices giving will not doubt "prove" their love for God through giving on other occasions. When such a situation occurs, that believer has no need to worry about being labeled as one who "robbed God." In like manner, one who gives the monetary equivalent to his or her tithe regularly also has no claim to "open windows" in heaven based on this act alone.

Consider this… The Scripture command that we not forsake the assembling of ourselves together (Hebrews 10:25). Yet, we understand the insanity of concluding that one who misses a week of church fellowship due to illness or even a family vacation will somehow be cursed of God unless they "make up the time." It's the heart of the servant that God is seeking and examining. Any ritualistic practice lacks the sincerity and heart felt sacrifice God requires for worship. With that, even legalistic tithing is a dishonor to God.

As givers, it is our pleasure to give our first and best back to God, according to His expectations throughout the dispensations (Psalm 96:8; 100; 150). For most, setting aside at least ten percent of one's income to give toward the work of ministry and the poor is a reasonable expectation (biblically and historically) that will ensure a spirit of giving (always rewarded by God) and consistently provide for the needs of the ministry and community. In this sense, the tithe should be a point of reference, or sanity check, for our giving, rather than a rule.

The Scriptures remind us that God loves a just (equal and accurate) balance (Proverbs 11:1). Knowing the truth of God's word teaches us to balance our obedience to the Law with the grace that has been extended to us through the blood of Jesus Christ. We must learn to bring God glory by being examples in the earth of integrity and love. This includes giving financially, though we must never lose sight of the many other requirements that complement our giving.

Our first priority is to worship. The foundation of pure worship is obedience. Obedience is only possible with knowledge. In all of our getting, we must then gain an understanding (Proverbs 4:7). Unfortunately, the issue of tithing is one that has plagued the modern-day church based on a foundation of ignorance and false testimony. It is not acceptable to receive all that has been taught, and repeat the same, without studying the Word of God – both Scripture and context. Tithing is not to be practiced as an act of Law. It is no longer required to receive favor from God. It is not required for salvation, nor favor from God. Failure to give, pay or honor a tithe does not result in unfavorable acts from God toward the believer. It is meant to provide for us, as are all other laws, a standard or discipline of behavior – a morally sound opportunity.

To put things simply, Jesus neither condemned nor encouraged tithing specifically for His disciples or the New Testament church. He did, however, state that He came to fulfill the Law, which will not pass away as long as the earth remains (Matthew 5:17-18). During His earthly ministry, He never discouraged tithing, but stressed only that it should be practiced within the proper context (2 Timothy 2:15). As faithful stewards and obedient followers of Jesus Christ, we must give cheerfully and secretly, as led of God and according to the order set in place by the founding Apostles, to whom power was delegated to build the church by Jesus Christ. As a result, our prayer is that our obedience in free will, grace giving, with the principles of tithing (sacrifice and proportion) as a pattern and standard, will be counted unto us as faith, just as it was for Abraham.

Furthermore, here [in the Levitical priesthood] tithes are received by men who are subject to death; while there [in the case of Melchizedek], they are received by one of whom it is testified that he lives [perpetually].

Hebrews 7:8, AMP

JOY ALLEN

CONCLUSION

Contextual history includes an account of evidence, proven by historical record, which surrounds the implementation and practice of a concept. We must understand where the practice of tithing originated and why the concept is included in Scripture altogether. Certainly, there must be a reason. Was this something God concocted only for those who followed Him, or was it a cultural aspect that was eventually exhibited among God's people?

A comprehensive study of the Scriptures proves that tithing was not initiated during the Law, nor originally mandated by God (that we can conclude through Scripture), as many are taught and believe. Throughout the dispensations, God has favored the tithe, or the tenth, of one's increase, though ceasing to require it in the dispensation of grace, which is that in which we currently live. Herein lies the argument we face today – does the absence of the mandate entitle us to conclude it no longer exists or does said absence simply imply the practice should have never ceased? This dispensation of grace, while it is not framed by Scriptures that clearly require the tithe, does indeed mandate relationship between God and the born-again believer. In any healthy relationship, both parties strive to do that which pleases the other, even when not mandated. With that, even if God doesn't require a tithe, can we not assume that it has pleased Him throughout time, and should therefore please Him now, if done with the right spirit? Can God and the tithe be likened unto a wife who has always loved white lilies? Her husband is aware that lilies are her favorite flower. Initially, she specifically requests them for her birthday. Yet, after some time, she makes no specific requests. To what extent is it her husband's responsibility to at least consider that she's always loved lilies and therefore provide them for special occasions?

To address our initial question – yes, a born-again believer should willingly *give*, applying the principles of the tithe, simply out of their love for God. It should be viewed as a gauge or benchmark, if you will, for giving as the Holy Spirit leads, with less emphasis on the amount and more on the motives of sacrifice and proportionate giving. Nonetheless, the obligation to *pay* a tithe is not only against the will of God, according to the Scriptures, but a damaging premise when taught by the New Testament church.

In today's church, the tithe is considered by many to approve or disprove of one's spiritual health, though the tithe, in and of itself is merely a physical offering. It is also used by many as a means of unlawful financial gain, demanding tithes and additional offerings of God's people. Many are being taught that to neglect a tithe yields curses while paying tithes consistently brings forth the favor of God, without any true consideration to other spiritual matters. This is the same type of teaching that Jesus openly condemned – one that stresses tithing while ignoring "weightier matters" that please God (Matthew 23:23). True worship should never be solicited through manipulation of the Scripture text, nor the purpose behind them.

An in-depth study of the tithe, through the history of God's word, clearly proves the tithe, once mandated as an act of the Law, is not to be relegated within the realm of grace as a law for modern-day believers. It does not, alone, yield curses or blessings from God. Yet it is a principle, guide or standard by which those who love God can demonstrate that love, from a financial perspective, through a method of worship already proven to please Him.

The truth of God's word brings freedom (John 8:32, 36), as we have been set free through Christ Jesus, our Messiah. In that freedom, we should purpose to give in a way that pleases our Father. We are instructed by the Holy Ghost to do that which is pleasing to Him without being bound to a law that threatens curses should we fail to comply.

We know this – true worship is a matter of the heart that cannot be judged by outward appearance. It is instead known only by God and discerned by others, through the Spirit of God, as He allows. Live holy. Hear God. Give freely and cheerfully. Quite simply, obey God (Ecclesiastes 12:13) and never allow yourself to be bound again! Selah.

BIBLIOGRAPHY

Dake, Fennis Jennings. *Dake Annotated Reference Bible, KJV*. Dake Publishing. 1999.

Kelly, Russell Earl, Ph.D. *Should the Church Teach Tithing? A Theologian's Conclusion about a Taboo Doctrine*. Writer's Club Press, 2007.

Lockman Foundation. *The Amplified Bible*. 1987.

Maehr, Jeffry T. *Tithing: Biblical or Not?* www.godkind.org/tithing. 1997-2008.

Merriam Webster, Inc. *Merriam-Webster Dictionary*. www.merriamwebster.com. 2014.

Powell, Mark Allen. *Harper-Collins Bible Dictionary-Revised*. HarperOne Publishing. 2011.

Ryrie, Charles. *Dispensationalism*. www.gotquestions.org, *"What are the seven dispensations?"* 2002-2014.

JOY ALLEN

ABOUT THE AUTHOR

Dr. Joy Allen, a native of Raleigh, NC, is called and anointed to train, equip and fortify leaders for the work of the ministry. She is a student of God's word, with a passion for Polemics and Apologetics. She also holds earned degrees in Foreign Language, Biblical Studies and Christian Ministry, having completed a Ph.D. in June 2014.

Joy is gifted and anointed to provide biblical training, mentoring, counseling, discipleship, instruction, commission/ordination, affirmation and spiritual counseling. Joy preaches a no-nonsense gospel of accountability, focusing heavily on building a solid, personal relationship with the Father through prayer and fasting, studying the Word and relying on the Holy Spirit to teach all things according to 1 John 2:20.

Dr. Allen, affectionately known as "Prophet Joy", serves alongside her husband as Apostle and co-Pastor at Breath of Life International Church, Founder and President of Joy of the LORD Ministries and a spiritual mentor to many, including a number of local pastors and leaders. By the grace of God, Dr. Allen is also the host of "Cry Aloud, Spare Not," a weekly prophetic radio broadcast.

Dr. Allen resides in North Carolina and is supported in ministry by her husband, Chris, and their two beautiful children, Jaaron and Jasmine, who are both active is ministry. Professionally, she enjoys a very successful career in Clinical Research. Truly, the favor of the Lord is upon her!

For more information about Joy Allen, visit
www.joyofthelordministries.org
www.breathoflifeintl.org

CURSED WITH A CURSE?